The Dragon Drawing War

This is a tale of two brothers, duelling to become a dragon drawing champion. Great sk[...] must be used to become the victor! If you don't succeed today, do not fear. There will be an[...] w[...] [...] tomorrow.

This picture book targets /r/ blends and is part of *Speech Bubbles 2*, a series of picture books that target specific speech sounds within the story.

The series can be used for children receiving speech therapy, for children who have a speech sound delay/disorder, or simply as an activity for children's speech sound development and/or phonological awareness. They are ideal for use by parents, teachers or caregivers.

Bright pictures and a fun story create an engaging activity perfect for sound awareness.

Picture books are sold individually, or in a pack. There are currently two packs available – *Speech Bubbles 1* and *Speech Bubbles 2*. Please see further titles in the series for stories targeting other speech sounds.

Melissa Palmer is a Speech Language Therapist. She worked for the Ministry of Education, Special Education in New Zealand from 2008 to 2013, with children aged primarily between 2 and 8 years of age. She also completed a diploma in children's writing in 2009, studying under author Janice Marriott, through the New Zealand Business Institute. Melissa has a passion for articulation and phonology, as well as writing and art, and has combined these two loves to create *Speech Bubbles*.

What's in the pack?

User Guide

Vinnie the Dove

Rick's Carrot

Harry the Hopper

Have You Ever Met a Yeti?

Zack the Buzzy Bee

Asher the Thresher Shark

Catch That Chicken!

Will the Wolf

Magic Licking Lollipops

Jasper the Badger

Platypus and Fly

The Dragon Drawing War

The Dragon Drawing War

Targeting /r/ Blends

Melissa Palmer

Routledge
Taylor & Francis Group

LONDON AND NEW YORK

First published 2021
by Routledge
2 Park Square, Milton Park, Abingdon, Oxon OX14 4RN

and by Routledge
52 Vanderbilt Avenue, New York, NY 10017

Routledge is an imprint of the Taylor & Francis Group, an informa business

British Library Cataloguing-in-Publication Data
A catalogue record for this book is available from the British Library

Library of Congress Cataloging-in-Publication Data
A catalog record has been requested for this book

ISBN: 978-1-138-59784-6 (set)
ISBN: 978-0-367-64888-6 (pbk)
ISBN: 978-1-003-12679-9 (ebk)

Typeset in Calibri
by Newgen Publishing UK

The Dragon Drawing War

Early in the **fr**osty morning,

We like to play a game,

Just my **br**other and I,

The **Dr**agon **Dr**awing War is its name.

We **gr**ab our pens and pencils,

We've **pr**actised the night before,

To **cr**eate the **tr**ickiest, **gr**andest, the **pr**ettiest,

Picture in the **dr**agon **dr**awing war!

Pens at the ready,

Gripping with all my might,

I **dr**aw a **gr**ey **fr**izzy-haired **dr**agon

Wearing a **dr**ess as black as night.

My **br**other **dr**ew his own **dr**agon,

As **gr**een as a tiny **gr**oss **fr**og,

With a **fr**ightful **fr**own it looked truly **cr**oss,

Crouching on a **br**oken log.

So I **dr**ew a **pr**owling **dr**agon,

Creeping **thr**ough **tr**ees without sound,

Gripping **br**anches with **cr**ackling talons,

Wings **dr**ooping on the **gr**ound.

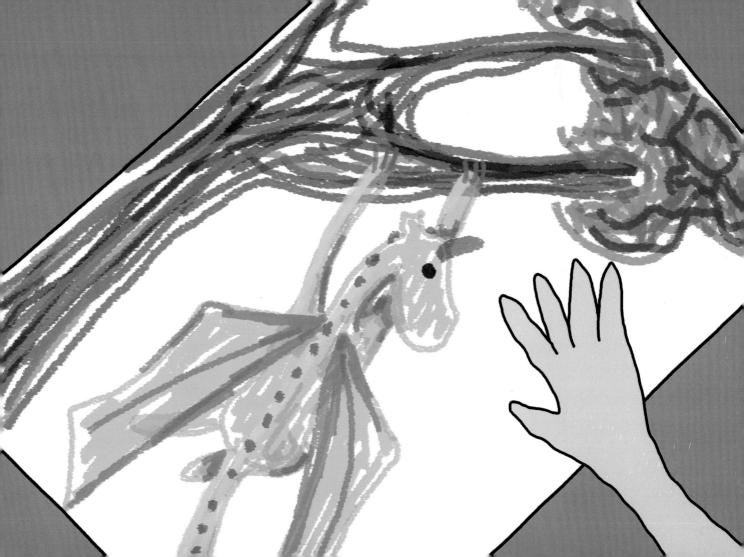

My **br**other stuck his tongue out,

Trying harder than ever before,

He **dr**ew a **gr**eat big **dr**agon

With giant **gr**een **gr**apes in its jaw!

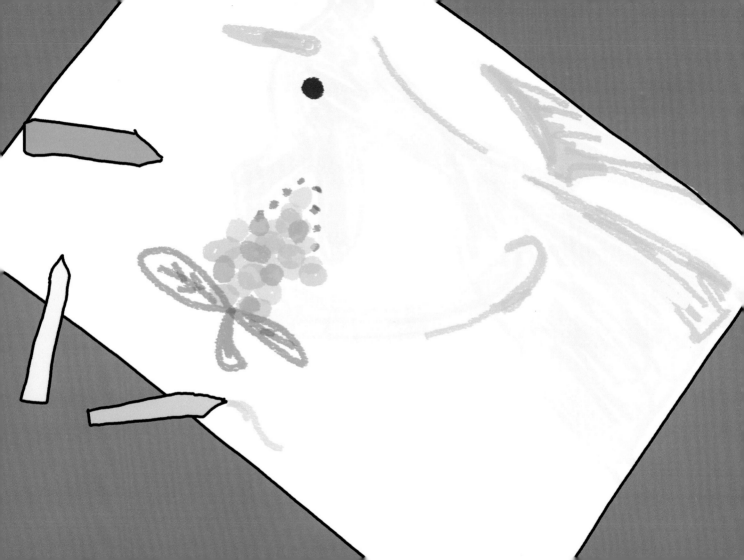

With a **gr**owl I started **dr**awing **-r-r-r-r-r-r-r-r-r-**

I reached deep into my **br**ain!

I **dr**ew a **pr**oud **gr**and **dr**agon

Driving a **pr**etty purple **tr**ain!

So my **br**other **dr**ew a **dr**agon

As a **pr**ince with a **cr**own on his head.

His face was rather **gr**aceful and peaceful

As he **dr**eamed, asleep in his bed.

"It's time for school!" Mum shouted.

"You must get **dr**essed and go!

Your **fr**iends are waiting to **dr**op you off.

You're going to be late, you know!"

So we ripped out our **dr**awings, **-r-r-r-r-r-r** rip,

From the paper pads and slapped them on the wall.

We **pr**omise to **dr**aw **dr**agons again really soon

Because we've had a ball.